Writing Practice

AGE 3-5

Sue Barraclough
Educational consultant: Margaret Deehan
Illustrated by Emma Holt

This workbook provides pre-writing and writing practice for young children. It should help your child:

- improve pencil control and boost confidence with pre-writing patterns and mazes
- improve hand – eye coordination
- understand the difference between drawing and writing
- become familiar with the 26 letter shapes
- understand that each letter shape has a sound
- become accustomed to reading and writing from left to right.

How to help your child

- Keep sessions short (about 20 minutes) and regular.
- The exercises are intended to be enjoyable as well as educational so always stop if your child is not relaxed or has lost concentration.
- Build confidence. Offer praise and encouragement for the smallest efforts. The exercises are simple but they are a challenge for a young child. It is important that they master basic skills thoroughly.
- Have at least four different coloured pencils or pens (preferably soft pencils or felt-tip pens) to do the exercises. Children will be able to see clearly what they have achieved and picking up and putting down pens is good practice. Give children plenty of room to practise – left-over wallpaper is ideal.
- Talk children through more complicated letters as they write them. The pages dealing with specific letters show how each letter should be formed. The letters are grouped according to starting points and similarities in shape and formation.
- Always use lower case letters, not capitals.
- Whenever possible encourage older children not to copy letters when they write them. Instead they should look carefully at the letter, say its sound, cover the letter, write it and then check if it is correct. This will be a useful skill when they are learning to spell later on.

Hodder
Children's
Books

NATIONAL CONFEDERATION OF · PARENT TEACHER ASSOCIATIONS ·

The only home learning programme supported by the NCPTA

Paint trails

Draw a coloured trail from the paint blob to the paint brush.

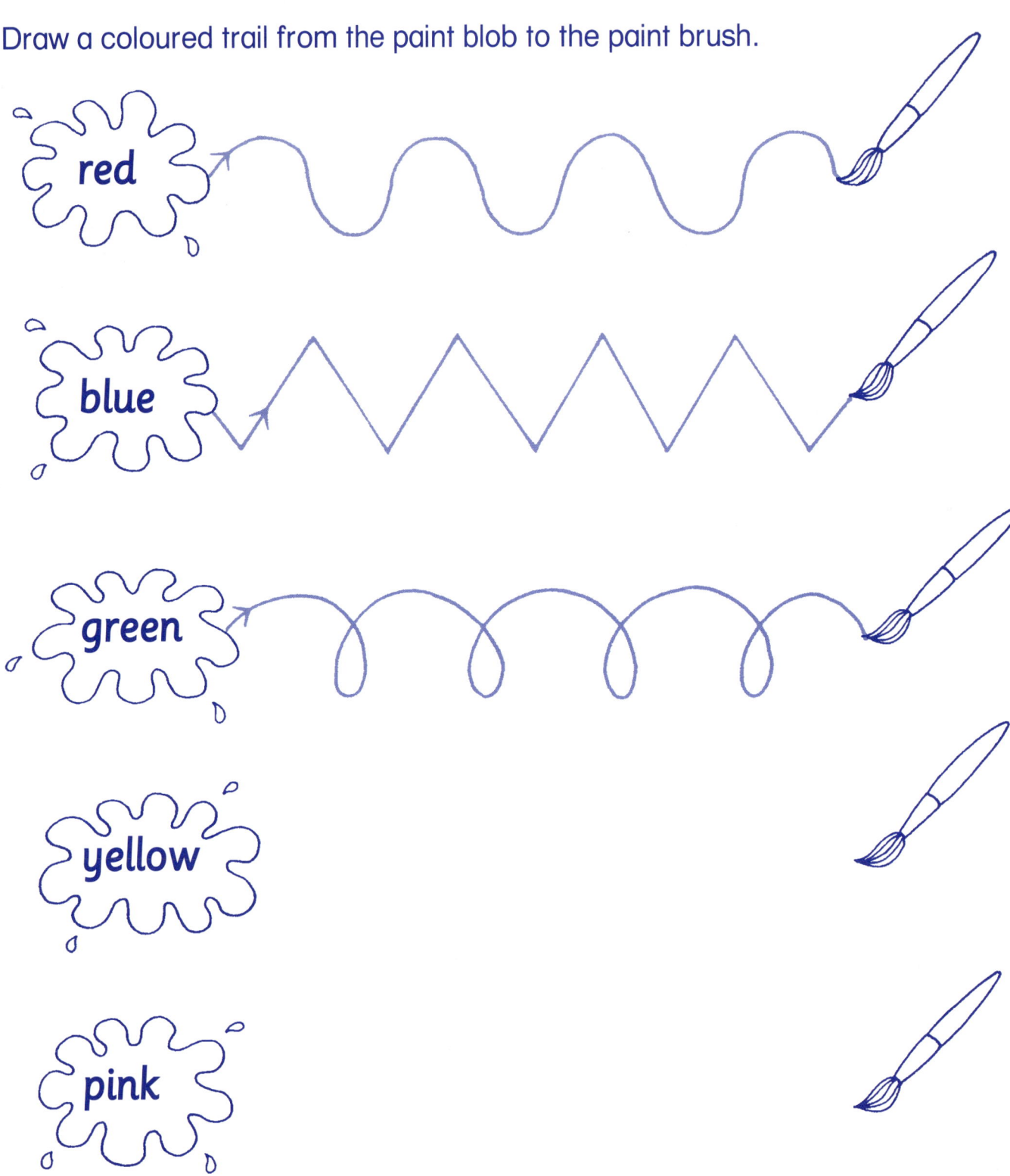

Same shape

Look at the first shape in each row, then make the other shapes match.

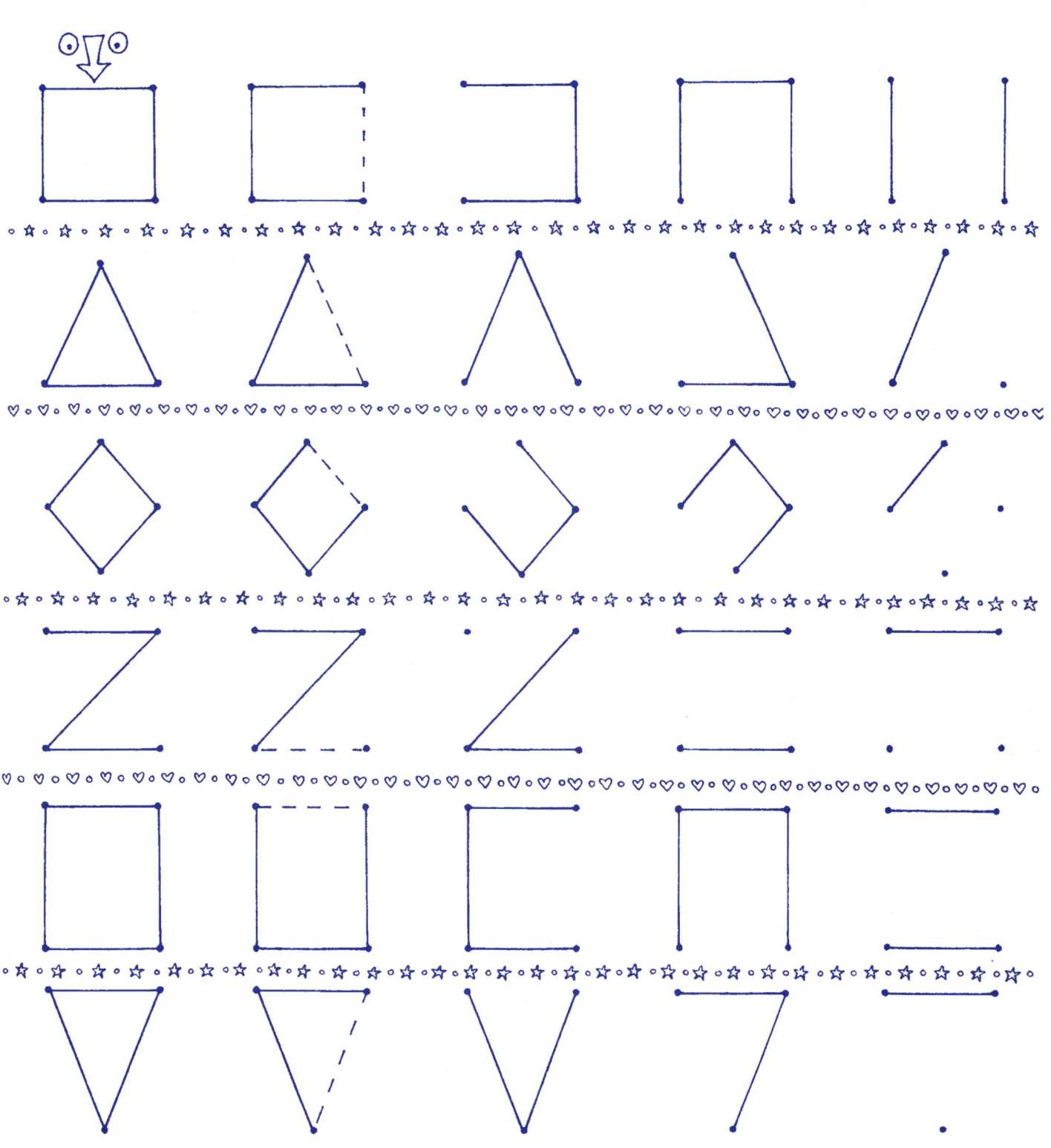

All the way home

Hansel and Gretel are lost in the woods. Use a blue pen
to follow Hansel's trail of stones to find their way home.

Use a red pen to draw Red Riding Hood's path through the woods.
Can you spot the Big Bad Wolf?

Goldilocks is running away from the three bears!
Can you show her the way home? Use a green pen this time.

Young children often find following paths difficult, so don't worry if they don't follow them exactly.

a, c, and o

Look carefully at each letter. Then draw a line to show which tower each block belongs to. Colour all the blocks in each tower the same colour.

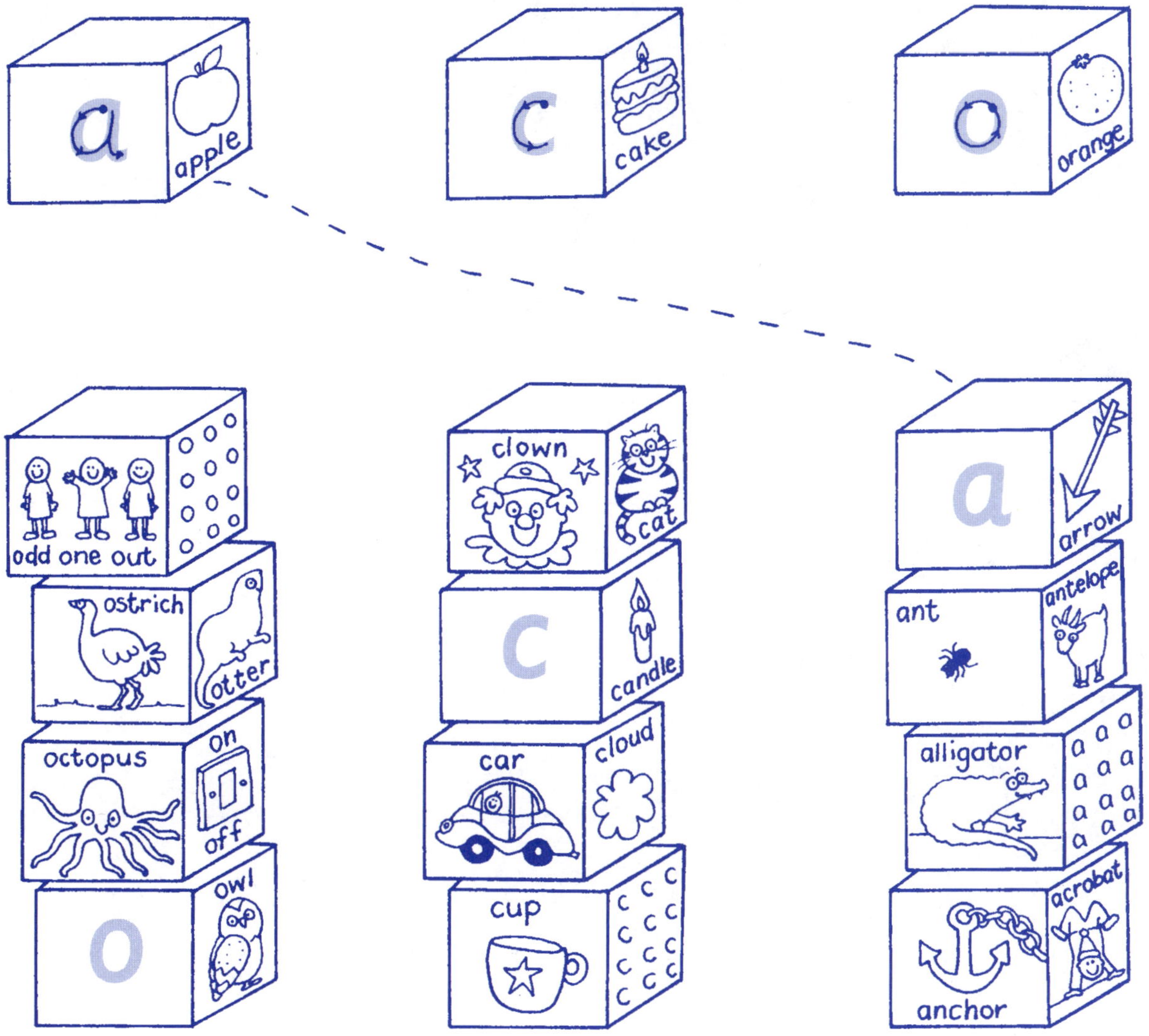

Now practise writing. Start at the dots ● and follow the arrows ↗.

This exercise involves matching letter shapes which is an important part of learning to write.
To do this, children need to find a particular letter shape in a jumble of pictures and letters.

Penguin paths

The penguins are playing in the ice and snow.
Draw over the penguins' paths.

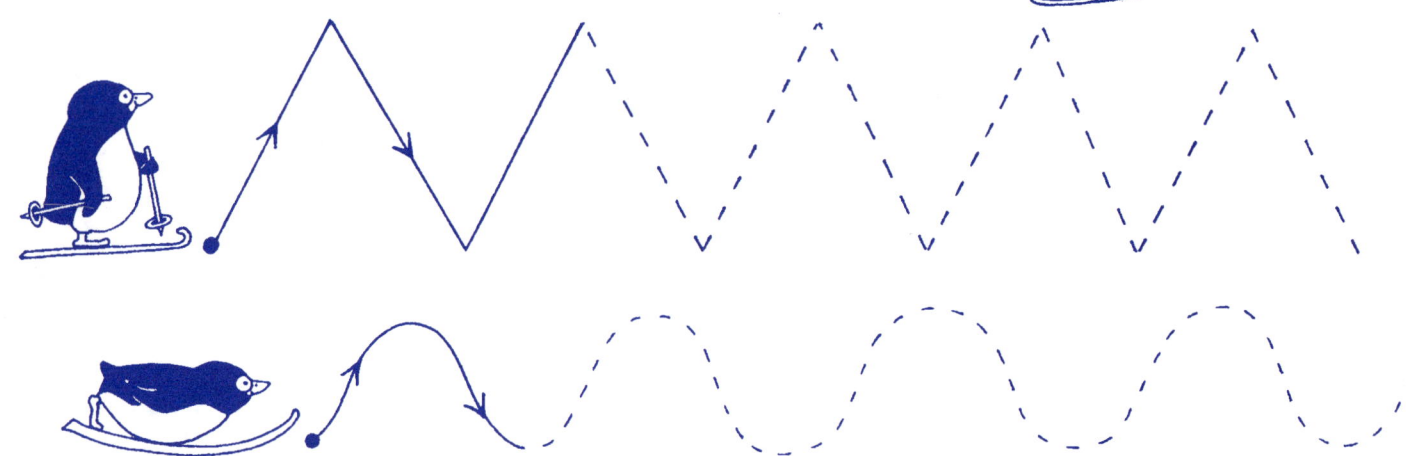

Draw each penguin's path right around the pond.

Draw a path going in and out of the icy igloos.

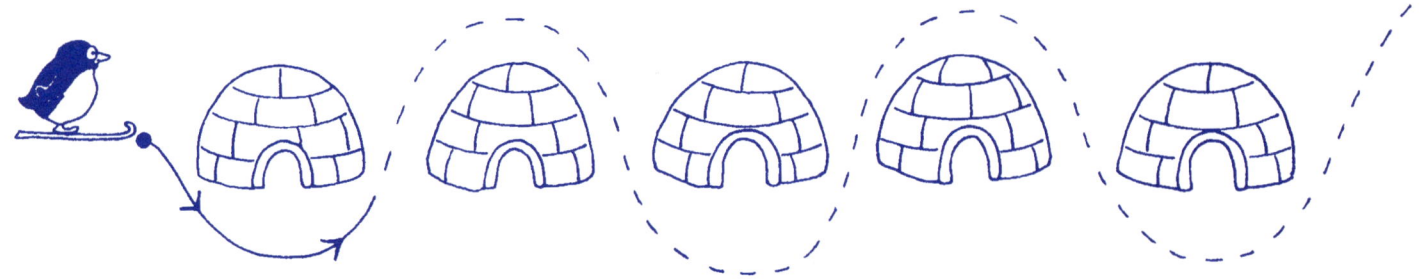

These exercises should continue to improve pen control.

d, g and q

Draw along each path from the dot ● to the cross ✗.
Keep your pen on the page all the way.
Use a different colour for each path.

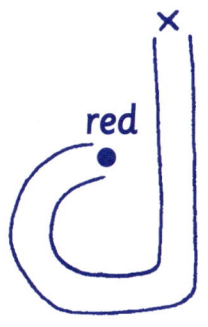

red

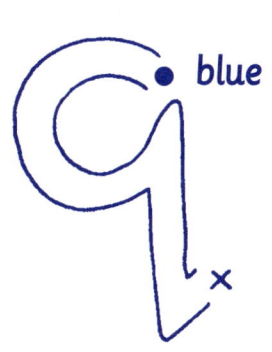

blue

orange

green

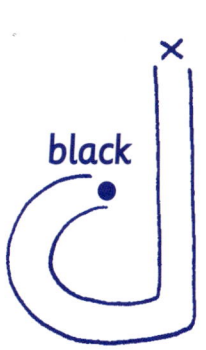

black

yellow

Now practise writing. Start at the dots ● and follow the arrows ↗.

d d g g q q

Patchwork patterns

Colour in the patterns on each patch.
Use lots of different colours.

b, h, and p

Look carefully at each letter. Then draw a line to show which tower each block belongs to. Colour all the blocks in each tower the same colour.

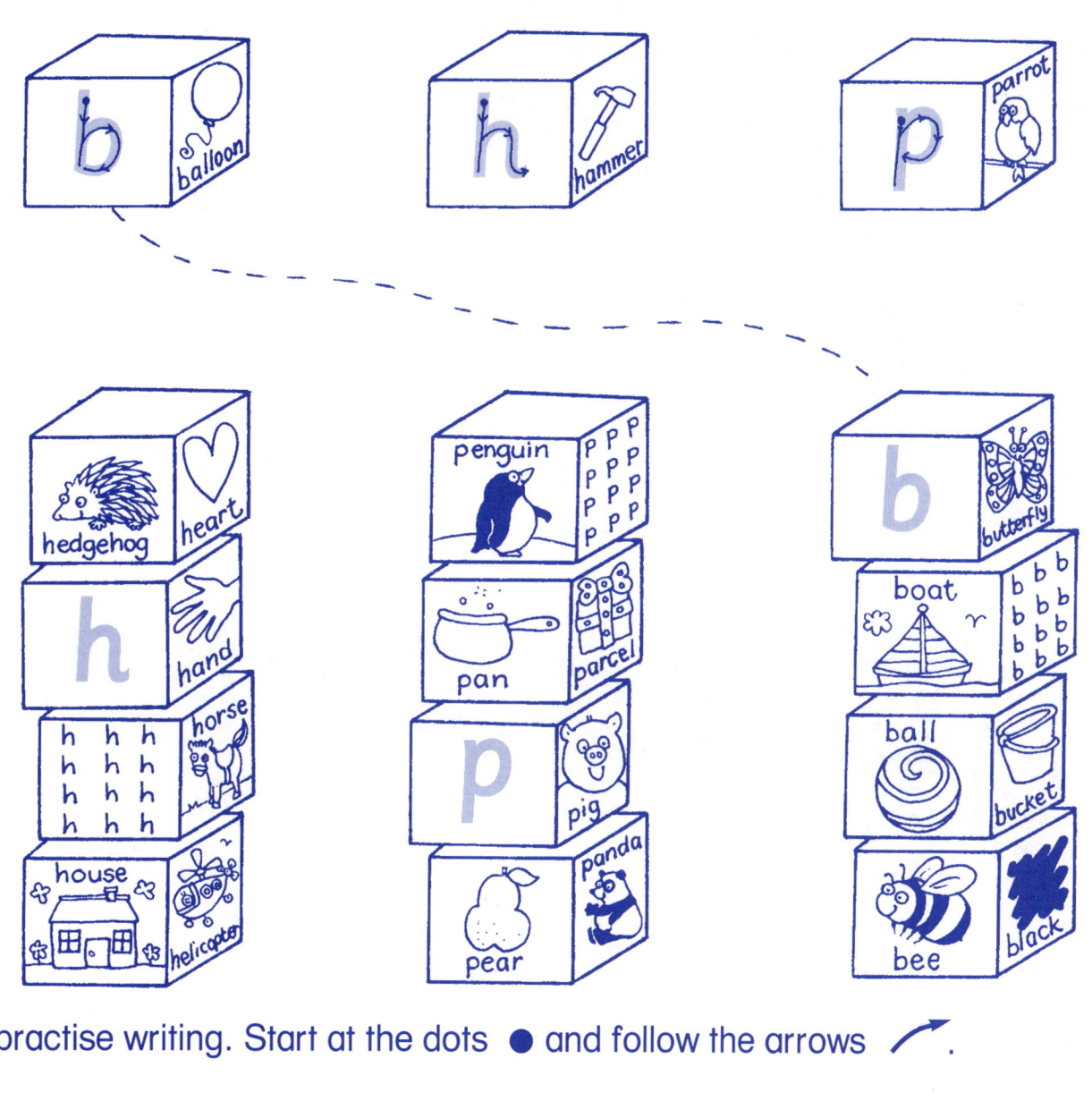

Now practise writing. Start at the dots ● and follow the arrows ↗.

b   b   h   h   p   p

Around and about

The rocket is zooming around the world.
Draw its path.

Draw the mouse's path
up the stairs.

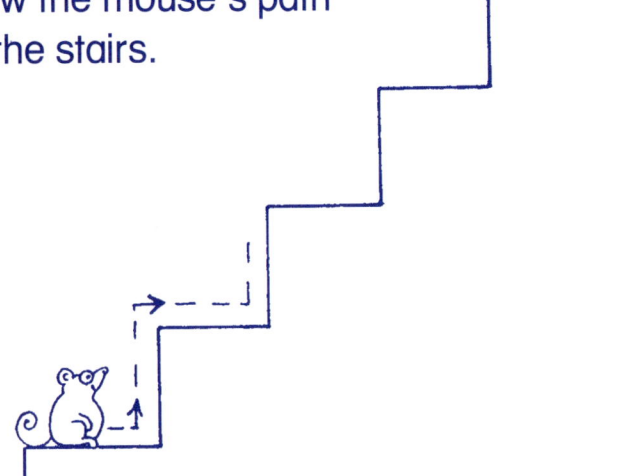

Draw steps
on the ladder.

Draw a path in and out of the bluebells.

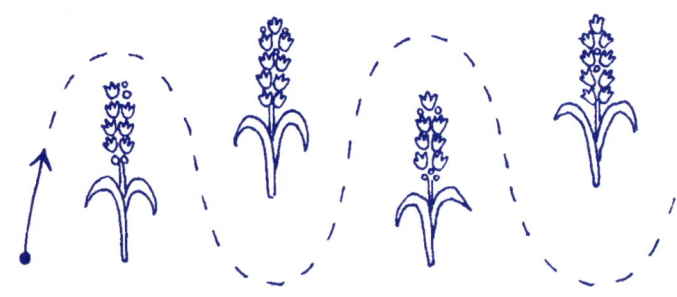

r, m, and n

Draw frog hops across the page.

Now draw rabbit hops. Make these hops higher.

Make the lamb's hops even higher – boing! boing!

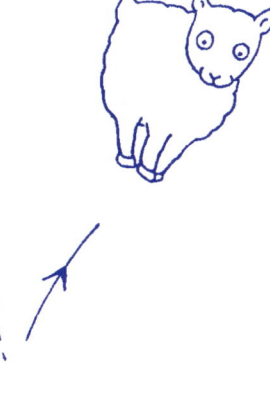

Now practise writing. Start at the dots ● and follow the arrows ⟋.

 r r  m  m n n

Hugs and kisses

Did you know an X means a kiss and an O means a hug?
Pretend this is a birthday card from you. Write your name
and then fill the rest of the card with hugs and kisses.

Happy Birthday

Hugs and Kisses
Love from

e and s

Look carefully at each letter. Then draw a line to show which tower each block belongs to. Colour all the blocks in each tower the same colour.

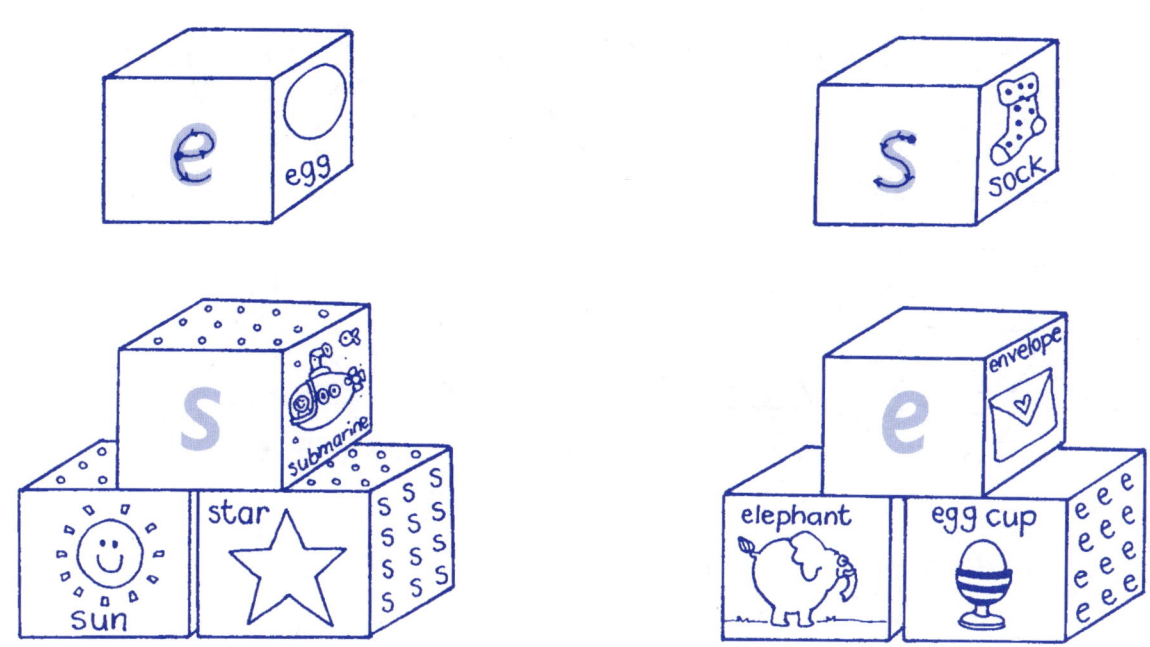

These snakes are making e and s shapes!
Colour the e snakes red and the s snakes blue.

Now practise writing. Start at the dots ● and follow the arrows ↗.

Patterns

Look carefully at each row. Can you finish each pattern?

i, j and l

  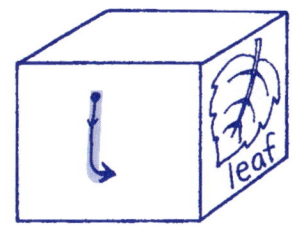

Draw stems for the flowers. Then colour the flowers red.

Draw trunks for the trees. Then colour the leaves green.

Now practise writing. Start at the dots ● and follow the arrows ↗.

i   i   j   j   l   l

These letters are very similar in formation and are relatively simple to write. If children can draw straight stems for the flowers they are doing well. Colouring is an important way of improving pen control.

f, k and t

Look carefully at each letter. Then draw a line to show which tower each block belongs to. Colour all the blocks in each tower the same colour.

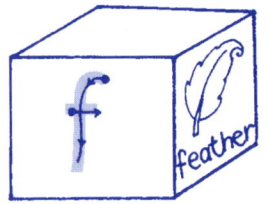

Now practice writing. Start at the dots ● and follow the arrows ↗.

Letter boxes

Look at the things in each box. Their names begin with the same letter.
Write this letter in the small box.

u and y

Draw over the dotted lines to finish the roundabout picture.
Then colour it brightly.

Now practise writing. Start at the dots ● and follow the arrows ↗.

u   u   u   y   y   y

Fancy dress

The children are dressed as their favourite animals.
Write an animal name on each box, then colour the costumes.

pig   bat   cat   hen

Here children are matching letters and writing whole words. See if they can write them without copying. Try using: Look–Say–Cover–Write–Check.

v, w, x and z

Look at each letter carefully. Then draw a line to show where each block belongs and colour the blocks to match.

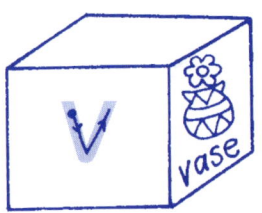   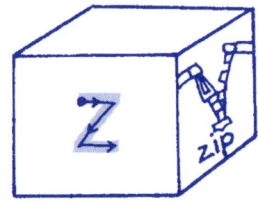

 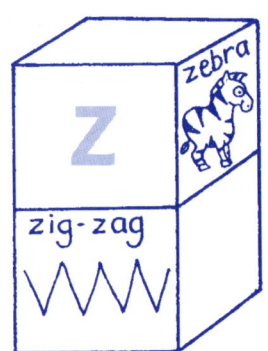  

Decorate one banner with zig-zags and one with crosses.

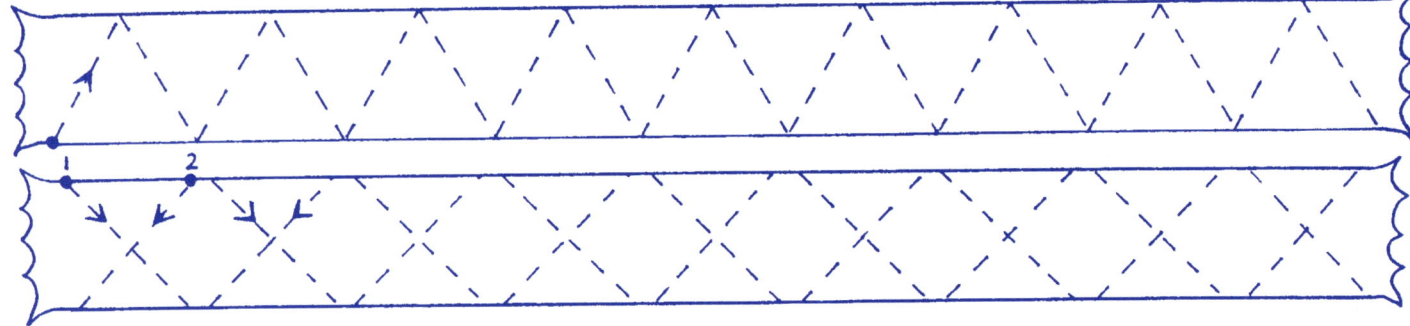

Now practise writing. Start at the dots ● and follow the arrows ↗.

a, e, i, o, u

Say each word and listen to the sound of the first letter.

apple   egg   igloo   orange   umbrella

Look at the picture and say each word carefully.
Draw lines to join the words that rhyme.
Then write the missing letters.

h e n

d i g

h o p

j u g

f a n

p __ g

p __ n

v __ n

m __ p

m __ g

Crazy golf

Can you find your way around the crazy golf alphabet course?
Draw the route around the course with a red pen,
using the alphabet at the bottom of the page to help you.

n o p q r s t u v w x y z

Rhyme time

hole   house   box   hat

Use the picture clues to find out which word to write
to finish each of the rhymes.

I am a fox
and I live in a _____ .

I am a mouse
and I live in a _____ .

I am a cat
and I live in a _____ .

I am a mole
and I live in a _____ .